T0131681

A BLUEPRINT FOR THE DAY

—

STARTING IT GOD'S WAY

SKYLAR BARRETT

WESTBOW
PRESS®
A DIVISION OF THOMAS NELSON
& ZONDERVAN

WestBow Press books may be ordered through booksellers or by contacting:

WestBow Press
A Division of Thomas Nelson & Zondervan
1663 Liberty Drive
Bloomington, IN 47403
www.westbowpress.com
844-714-3454

ISBN: 978-1-6642-5632-3 (sc)
ISBN: 978-1-6642-5631-6 (hc)
ISBN: 978-1-6642-5630-9 (e)

Library of Congress Control Number: 2022901789

Print information available on the last page.

WestBow Press rev. date: 2/22/2022

CONTENTS

DEDICATION

I dedicate this book to my better half, my best friend, my sweet and precious bride. Thank you for your encouragement, your confidence in me, your undeniable love. I am the man I am today because of your love and the way you point me closer to Jesus every day. Thank you for all you do!

I also dedicate this book to my two sons, Matthew and Benjamin. It is such a privilege and honor to be your father. You two radiate God's love and joy, thank you for being such wonderful boys!

ABOUT THE AUTHOR

Hi, my name is Skylar Barrett. I love my Lord and Savior Jesus, my gorgeous wife Ashleigh and my wonderful sons Matthew and Benjamin. I am passionate about enjoying this life God has given us and sharing that passion with others. I have the privilege of leading an amazing team at a consulting technology firm as well as building out a dream ministry with my wife at Mustard Seed Faith Investments. My family and I believe in THINKING BIG, LOVING BIG and GIVING BIG. Our heart and passion are for generosity. We stand on Proverbs 11:24 (MSG) that "the world of the generous gets larger and larger, and the world of the stingy gets smaller and smaller."

This is my first book that I have written, and I am so humbled that you are reading it. With this being my first book, I wanted to follow the example of one of my favorite authors Robert Morris (author of the Blessed Life and Beyond

Blessed) and I am committing to pour all the book sales back into our ministry at Mustard Seed Faith Investments. My wife and I believe God gave us this book as a first fruits to sow back into our ministry and impact His kingdom here on earth.

I pray that this book and this blueprint for your day will have as much of an impact on your life as it has on mine while following it. I am excited to connect with you, learn your story, pray with and for you and learn how this book has affected your life. Reach out to me through mustardseedfaithinvestments.com

THE SCRIPTURE LIST

Matthew 6:9-13

Matthew 6:33-34

Romans 12:12

Romans 13:11-12

Ephesians 6:10-17

1 Peter 2:24

Matthew 10:8

Hebrews 4:12-13

Deuteronomy 28:1-2

Deuteronomy 28:15

James 1:5-6

Psalm 91:1-16

Matthew 11:28-30

Psalm 92: 1-2

Psalm 98:1

Psalm 139:23-24

James 1:19

Proverbs 18:21

James 5:16

Proverbs 4:23-27

PREFACE

"I've come to terms with the fact that I'll never be ready for anything God has called me to. And that's OK. God doesn't' call the qualified; He qualifies the called." - Mark Batterson (author of Circle Maker)

This quote from Mark has stuck with me over the years as I have felt the calling from the Lord and have heard from others that I should write a book. I'm not traditionally qualified to write a book, I am not an author, that isn't a skill or a talent I have been working on for years. Trust me when I say, I did not think I was qualified or would be able to write a book. But, just as Mark said, that was okay. I didn't need to be qualified; God would do that for me. He would give me the ideas and the words. And it was probably the one thousandth time I read that quote and then heard from the Lord, "write a book Skylar". It finally happened. God had qualified me. He had so graciously given me this idea for the book. He then carved out the time and the space for it. He started to download specific ideas day in and day out while confirming those ideas through my wife, through my pastors, and through listening to other wise counsel.

We are living with distractions, concerns, noise of the news and the loud opinions of people around us that God wanted to remind us He has a plan to combat all of it. A plan to make sense of it and to give us reprieve. That plan is what He gave and is what this book is all about: A Blueprint for the day, Starting it God's way.

I am so excited to share this blueprint for the day with you. I know it will impact your life in a wonderful way but truthfully, I am even more excited to be using this myself. Following this plan changed my days. It has brought me more joy; it has drawn me closer to the Lord and it has positively affected my health greatly. I start the day excited to wake up and I feel more energized (even though I am sleeping less hours). My daily interactions with my family, friends, and co-workers are more impactful and meaningful. I am making better decisions at work because

I have asked and received wisdom. I am seeing God work in new ways because I am anticipating and looking for them during the day.

To sum it up, this blueprint has given me a better mindset, a softer heart, and a healthier body.

I am excited to hear how this blueprint affects you, the changes you see, and the ways God works in you and in your family's lives. I believe the Lord will use this to qualify you for the things He has in store, plans that only He can accomplish through your obedience.

INTRODUCTION

Whether you recognize it or not, the Bible is the most important book ever written. It is vital to read it, understand it, meditate on it, and put it to use. It's the story of our true family's history and it's our Father's will for our lives both literally and metaphorically. We should be memorizing it, personalizing it, sharing it, and most importantly speaking it out loud daily and often.

If you listen to successful individuals, they will tell you the most important part of the day is the morning. The act of waking up early, setting yourself in the right mindset, getting your body moving and preparing for the day is what separates the great lives from the average lives. This is true whether you are a disciple of Jesus or not. It's a universal truth and has been since the beginning of creation.

This combination of diving into scripture, spending time talking to the Father, and exercising to begin the day is the blueprint to a successful day and life. The days I choose to follow this blueprint are always the most gratifying, successful, and peaceful days. It sets up my entire day and not just for myself, but for my wife and kids, as well as my teams at work and those who I do life with around me. As a leader in my household, my job and in my community, it is imperative I start my day on the right foundation so that everyone around me can benefit from it.

At this point in my life and in my journey as a follower of Christ and as a leader, I wanted to share this blueprint.

There are two aspects of this blueprint that don't need much explanation or detail. First, get up early (and I mean early) and secondly, do some type of exercise. That exercise can range from an intense workout to just walking, the point here is not for physical fitness, it's the act of getting your body moving and prepared for the day. As an example, I wake up every day at 5:00 am. and my workouts range from fifteen-minute walks to thirty-minute intense core workouts. Waking up your body with exercise directly wakes up your mind as well and doing this as early as possible sets you up for the day.

Now, the third aspect to this blueprint is the time dedicated to the Lord, both in prayer and in reading scripture. This is the part of the plan that I ignored for over thirty-two years, by not prioritizing it or understanding the importance of it. And importance is not even the right word. This part of the plan is so vital to truly having breakthrough in your life and creating the opportunity for successful days, each and every day.

Let me take a quick second to describe what I mean by a successful day. Because it's not what the world would necessarily describe as successful. It doesn't mean just these things: easy going, lucky, nothing bad happened, people were kind to you, you felt great, you made good money, got a promotion, etc. Those things are great but that's settling in my book, and I truly believe that's settling according to the Good Book, The Bible. I'm not settling in this life for a good day according to the world's standards. God has promised us in His Word the opportunity for divinely amazing days. Days full of peace, joy, gladness, protection against the enemy physically/emotionally/spiritually, prosperity in spirit and in our finances, and health in our bodies. An Abundant Life. That's the successful days I am talking about, and God has shown me through His Word, the blueprint he laid out for us to experience all our days.

When trying something new or establishing a new habit, as I am about to encourage you to do, it starts with two things and continues each day with a third element. First is having faith in that this new habit you are creating or this new thing you are trying will work. Second, is starting. It's planting the seed into this new habit. Thirdly, and what is continual, is watering and caring for the seed or the new habit you started. Letting it grow and change the environment around it (in this sense, this is your life). The act of doing this is what will start to change your life. This new habit will bring these successful days I am speaking about, where after a while you get to start reaping the harvest of the habit and truly experiencing what God said we get to daily in His Word. The Abundant Life.

Jump in and join me in this blueprint for our lives. Set that alarm, get out of bed, get moving, grab that Bible and notepad, and most of all expect your day to change. Because God wants your day to be successful and for your life to flourish, He just wants it to start with Him!

CHAMPIONS ARE
MADE AT 5 AM

The correlation between waking up early and being successful is something that has been known to be true since the beginning of time and throughout all cultures. When you meet truly successful and fulfilled individuals, you will find they are all early risers. They will set their alarms just to be prepared, but 90 percent of the time, they wake up before the alarm sounds. I discovered this is the case because they are excited to start the day. There is an urgency to attack the morning so that they can be successful during the day. I learned this from observing successful individuals and from being taught it by my mentors at a young age. Therefore, I made the choice to adopt this habit right out of college, and it has paid off in spades.

When you ask others in my life to describe me, they often use terms such as *joyful, prepared, ahead of the game,* and *relaxed.* I often get the question, "where do you get the time to get all the things done that you do?" I can attribute these accolades largely to my habit of getting up early and the benefits that transpire from that. Before most people have had their first cup of coffee, I have already spent time with the Lord, exercised, caught up on all work items and personal email, spent quality time with my wife and kids, and have laid plans for the day. What I find even more clear is when I am having an off day or a bad attitude, that day usually began with a bad morning where I didn't wake up early and do the things I mentioned previously.

I have chosen 5:00 a.m. as the ideal time to wake up. No matter if it's summer or winter, it's before the sunrise (which is an extra benefit—believe me when I say sunrises will become your favorite), and it gives me the opportunity to accomplish all the things I need to before any other expectations of me arise. That part is important because as a husband, a father, and a leader in my workplace, I have a lot of expectations and responsibilities, and I need to be at my best to rise to those.

To those who consider themselves night owls and not morning people, I have a word and a challenge for you. I understand it can be seen to be just as effective to have your quiet time and time with the Lord in the evenings after everything has calmed down. You will say this is the time where you can actually be alone with the Lord and read and reflect. But let me challenge you with a thought on that. The evening, before you go to bed might be a good time to reflect, but it's just that, its reflecting. It doesn't provide you the opportunity to take God's Word and let it impact you immediately throughout the day. It doesn't set up your day and start it with communicating with God first. So, I challenge you to challenge your current mindset. Try this morning routine for 60 days, see if it doesn't change your perspective and affect your day in a way that will make you a morning person for the rest of your life.

If I have learned anything in thirty-four years of life, it's that waking up early and starting the day right is what creates the foundation for a successful life. As further proof and evidence that this isn't just my thoughts, below are quotes from successful and well followed individuals about the importance and practice of waking up early.

Now in the morning, having risen a long while before daylight, He went out and departed to a solitary place; and there He prayed.
—Mark 1:35 (NKJV)

5 am to 8 am are "The Golden Hours" and the most successful achievers in the world use these hours to set up their days for success. The way you begin your day really does determine how you live your day.
—Robin Sharma, bestselling author

On rising early: getting up early and acknowledging that since God knows my heart better than myself, He must know what is best for every aspect of my life.
—Jared Madrazo, former Army Officer

It is well to be up before daybreak,
for such habits contribute to
health, wealth, and wisdom.
—Aristotle

The sun has not caught me
in bed in fifty years.
—Thomas Jefferson

Champions are made at 5 am.
—Michael Jordan

Wake up early and tackle the day before it
tackles you. Be on offense, not defense.
-Evan Carmichael, Author
and Venture Capitalist

Early to bed and early to rise makes a
man healthy, wealthy, and wise.
—Benjamin Franklin

An early-morning walk is a
blessing for the whole day.
—Henry David Thoreau

My voice You shall hear in the morning,
O Lord; In the morning I will direct
it to You, And I will look up.
—Psalm 5:3 (NKJV)

SCRIPTURE TIME

Reading scripture is the most important element in the blueprint for the day. There are entire books and studies that go into detail about the reason behind this, but I am going to do my best to explain it in a few pages.

Scripture is important because it contains God's will for our lives. The Bible is full of guidelines, commandments, directions, and encouragements that give us concrete and flawless insight into God's will for us in every aspect of life. One of the most prolific authors of the Bible, Paul, writes in 2 Timothy 3:16 (NKJV) that "all scripture is given by inspiration of God, and is profitable for doctrine, for reproof, for correction, for instruction in righteousness, that the man of God may be complete, thoroughly equipped for every good work." How amazing is it that the Bible is inspired by God Himself! It's His Word, holding His directions and wisdom,

His goodness, His intentions for us as His children, and ultimately His heart for us.

Secondly, Scripture is the most vital nourishment for the day. It's not food or water that we need the most; it's the Word that nourishes our very spirits and souls. I have learned that my body and mind are truly healthier when I feed my soul and spirit with the Word first. The best companion to water, food, and vitamins is the Word of God. It is written in Matthew 4:4 (NKJV), "man shall not live by bread alone, but by every word that proceeds from the mouth of God." There are a lot of words in the Bible, and if God says every word proceeds from His mouth, then taking some of it in each day is a good start.

One of my favorite things about reading scripture each morning is that it gives me discernment for the day. We know that the Word of God is living and powerful, that it is sharper than a sword, and that it will discern our thoughts and the intent of our heart. The Bible will discern our thoughts and the intentions of our own hearts—that is amazing and humbling! I have realized that as human beings, it is so natural to seek our own or some expert's opinion. But still, it remains so hard for us to discern between what is good and what is bad. Our natural judgments are often tainted by the world and our personal opinions, emotions, and experiences that go against God's good and perfect will. But how good is God that He gives us His Word and that His Word cuts through all of this. It separates out all self-seeking in our lives and decides what is actual truth and righteousness.

The Passion Translation says it so well in Psalm 92:6. David says, "such amazing mysteries found within every miracle that nearly everyone seems to miss. Those with no discernment can never really discover the deep and glorious secrets hidden in your ways." Every morning, even though I read the same scriptures, I will discover something new, some revelation God wants me to learn—as it says above, His secrets for my life. It's this revelation that I am excited for you to gain when you embark on this plan.

Scripture also answers a great question that David asks in Psalm 119:9 (NKJV): "how can a young man cleanse his way? By taking heed according to Your word." We know how important scripture is when we go back to what Timothy said in chapter 3:16–17 (NKJV): "all scripture is given by inspiration of God, and is profitable for doctrine, for reproof, for correction, for instruction in righteousness." The Bible contains all the instruction that we need to create a life that is full of righteousness and one that we and those around us will be proud of.

Above all, a great reason to read Scripture is that it is full of God's promises. God's Word speaks of all the marvelous things that belong to those who love and trust Him. The key word there is *belong*. When we choose to follow Jesus and choose a life of obedience and dedication to Him, then as His children, we get to take part in the blessings and become part of the family. We belong to Him and His family! There are more promises than you can imagine that God makes to those who live according to His will. So, the question that begs to be answered is, do you want to see what God does, and will do, for those who live according to His will? If so, pick up your Bible with me. It will lay out all the promises that can be yours, both in this life and in eternity.

The following chapters are based off the scriptures that this plan calls out to read each morning. The order of the passages is significant, as throughout my journey of this blueprint, the Lord has added scripture and has ordered them accordingly. The passages of scripture are listed in the back of the book in the same order so you can reference them easily each morning.

THE LORD'S PRAYER

In this manner, therefore, pray:
Our Father in heaven,
Hallowed be Your name.
Your kingdom come.
Your will be done
On earth as it is in heaven.
Give us this day our daily bread.
And forgive us our debts,
As we forgive our debtors.
And do not lead us into temptation,
But deliver us from the evil one.
For Yours is the kingdom and the
power and the glory forever. Amen.
—Matthew 6:9–13 (NKJV)

I began reading this passage each morning exactly as it is written, but soon after, the Lord directed me to use it as a model of prayer, so I started expanding on it as the Lord led. For example, as it says, "forgive us our debts," I started repenting and asking for forgiveness for specific sins I had committed. Likewise, as it says, "do not lead us into temptation," I said out loud the ways I knew I was tempted to do the wrong things, then I declared that I would not fall into those traps and that the enemy had no power over me. I reminded myself that the kingdom and the power belong to God, not the enemy. The act of saying this out loud gives more authority to the words.

This passage should be the first one to be read because it speaks to the importance of being in the Word every day. Give us today our daily bread. When I read this, I say to the Lord, give me today my daily bread, your scripture, so that I can seek forgiveness, extend forgiveness, resist temptation, flee from the enemy and remember that God holds all the power. The latter part of this passage is available to us because we have spent time reading, understanding, and applying His Word in our lives.

This passage is a declaration to start the day. It was the very way Jesus told his disciples, his closest friends on this earth, how to pray. Each sentence is an aspect and a reminder of what should be on our mind during the day and in what order. The order is the most important aspect in my opinion.

It starts with praise, thanksgiving, recognizing God is in control. It's His will be done, not ours. Then it's a reminder, there is a heaven, there is an eternity. It's not all about our time on this earth. We need to have a heavenly mindset and ask God to do what is in heaven, in our lives on earth. To further cement this truth in your life, start to declare that God does what is in heaven not just on earth but in your own state, your city, and your own home. There is power in personalizing the Word of God.

God brings our attention to His word, our daily bread. As it says, man does not live on bread and water alone, but on every word from the Lord. We need to be in the scripture daily, hence this blueprint to a successful *day*. Now, we are brought to repentance, the chance to seek forgiveness from the Lord for our failings, for being selfish and for the hurts we have caused others. Just as important, is that we need to forgive others. We often forget this part. However, God makes it clear in His Word, that He will not forgive us if we haven't forgiven others. Read that again. Because that is a humbling notion.

God then makes it clear that we need to remember there is an evil one. We don't fight against flesh and blood but against Satan, who is the evil one. That we need to seek God's help to fight against temptation. Lastly, God brings us back to the reality that He is number one, He deserves the honor and the glory and most importantly He has the power.

Starting with this passage positions me in the right frame of mind. It sets my priorities straight allowing me to begin the day as the Lord intended, the very way Jesus started His mornings. By the time I am done repeating this scripture and mediating on it, I have given God praise, asked for His forgiveness, removed all unforgiveness in my heart towards others, and told the enemy as I like to say, to pound sand, that He has no control over me. God is who maintains the power.

SEEK FIRST

*But seek first the kingdom of God and
His righteousness, and all these things
shall be added to you. Therefore do not
worry about tomorrow, for tomorrow will
worry about its own things. Sufficient
for the day is its own trouble.*
-Matthew 6:33-34 (NKJV)

But seek first the Kingdom of God. These were the words that were spoken to my wife and I while we were being prayed over at the Church on the Rock in Bunnell, Florida this past summer. One of the pastors there, had just prophesied over us the amazing plans the Lord has for our lives. Plans that were magnificent, that held details consisting of blessings from God of outpouring financial and physical gifts to my family. But she followed up those words with saying "the Lord wants you above all and first and foremost to seek Him first, seek the Kingdom of God first and Skylar and Ashleigh all these things that I spoke of will be added to you". After hearing this, I spent time truly grasping to understand what does seeking the kingdom of God look like in practicality because He made it clear through the words of that pastor that He wanted my wife and I to know this truth.

What I came to find is that apparently, God wants all His children to know the importance of seeking FIRST His Kingdom. The Kingdom of God is mentioned more than eighty times in the New Testament. A good portion of Jesus's teachings revolve around the Kingdom of God. It was a topic He taught on many times. God wants us to experience His kingdom not only in heaven but in this life as well. As you read this passage each day, take time to ask the Lord, what do you want me to learn about your kingdom today. Then get ready to turn the pages in your Bible because He will begin to lead you to other passages that give revelation to this question.

The second part of this passage speaks to the worries and concerns that we as humans deal with daily. Earlier in the book of Matthew,

Jesus mentions that what we shall not worry about what we eat or what we shall wear for the day. But we all know additionally there is a long list of other things we worry ourselves about. These worries and concerns too often consume our lives and for the most part the sad thing is that most of these worries and concerns never materialize into anything. So, in the grand scheme of things, it ends up being a waste of time and energy. Jesus knew this would be the case so that's why He tells us to not worry about these things and do not worry about tomorrow either. Then the question becomes, then what shall we do? Well, good thing Jesus answered that in that we shall seek first the kingdom of God and then all those things we worry and concern ourselves with will be taken care of.

At first that sounds too good to be true. But let me tell you from experience that since I have taken this passage to heart, I have seen this manifest itself to be true. Each day I seek him first and seek what His Kingdom means for me that day and then my day and my concerns are taken care of. Very quickly you will start to understand that God wants us seeking His Kingdom because he truly intended for us to experience heaven on earth. That includes peace that overcomes you in the best way. It us confidence that you are loved by God for who He made you to be. As you seek Him first, your eyes will be opened throughout the day to see how He is working in all things, in ways you have missed your entire life. I can only compare it to the stark difference in walking through a forest trail in the dark compared to walking it in broad day light. Night and day. Jesus is true to His word. What He says plainly in the Bible is truth and that goes for this as well. If we will seek His kingdom first, before we start our day and not seek our own needs, He will be true to His word and He will take care of our needs. Try it for yourself and see how it plays out to be true. Then write down those specific ways so you can refer to them in the future as encouragement and as a testimony to others.

MY LIFE'S VERSE

Be joyful in hope, patient in
affliction, faithful in prayer.
-Romans 12:12 (NIV)

For this passage in Romans, I use the NIV version only because that is how I memorized it years ago as this has been my life verse since I was around thirteen. I read it as it is written, then I expand on what I am hopeful for today, for the future, and for everything I have hope for in my life. Then I seek his patience and declare I will be patient. I then say out loud all the afflictions that are happening in my family's life right now, reminding myself and declaring to the Lord that I will be faithful to bring these things to Him in prayer throughout the day.

"Hope deferred makes the heart sick," is something my wife will refer to when a situation has seemed to become hopeless for someone. Hope is defined as a feeling of expectation and desire for a certain thing to happen. It's a universal thing, no matter which culture, hope plays a vital role. As the saying above goes, if there isn't hope, one does truly feel helpless and even sick. That's why as someone who follows Jesus, it is so amazing to have true hope. Through Jesus, hope changes its definition from desire to certainty. Our hope in Jesus promises us eternal life, plans to prosper and to keep us from harm and the promise that He is in control. Every morning when I read this scripture, I recite all the things I am hopeful for, and certain of, and I do it with joy. I do it with a smile on my face. I am confident that when you take on this habit, this blueprint for the day, and recite this verse each morning, your joy and hope will be clear to all around you. You will feel lighter and more apt to tackle the day with vigor.

Next comes patience, everyone's favorite fruit of the spirit. That might be a little bit of a stretch, but I believe practicing and having patience is a true separator in this life. Those whom as this verse says can be patient in affliction, are the ones who lead, are the encouragers, are the ones who build ministries and businesses, and are the ones you count on when it matters most. Every day comes with its challenges. Even Jesus said that was the case when He said today has enough problems for itself. So, if that's the case, then being able to be patient while going through those troubles would be a key attribute to take on. Reading this each day will help keep patience at the top of your mind. I promise you after reading this day after day, you will start to practice patience in trials, and you will see the fruit that comes from it. It will also be clear to others thus providing you an opportunity to share the why behind your newfound patience which leads to a golden chance to credit God and share the Gospel.

Faithful in prayer or as some translations say, steadfast in prayer. This one is self-explanatory, be consistent in your prayer life. The easiest way for me to do this is to remember what prayer is in its simplest form, a conversation with God. That's right, prayer is talking to God, your savior, your best friend, your heavenly father. It should come in all forms; it should be formal and be done in a secret place, it should be corporate and with your family, it should be done while driving, or while working. I believe it should mimic our most treasured earthly relationships and how we communicate in those. We know for a relationship to be effective, it needs great communication, and prayer is just that, communicating with God. So, let's practice that and thus be faithful and steadfast in our prayer.

FOR A TIME, SUCH AS NOW

And do this, understanding the present time: The hour has already come for you to wake up from your slumber, because our salvation is nearer now than when we first believed. The night is nearly over; the day is almost here. So let us put aside the deeds of darkness and put on the armor of light.
-Romans 13:11-12 (NKJV)

As I was sitting in a prayer service earlier this year, the Lord brought the above passage to my attention and told me that as a society we are in a season right now where we need to recognize the time and need to daily do what this passage says; to cast off the works of darkness and be the armor of light. Just as God blinded Saul with light and he turned from his dark ways and turned to the Lord, so are we to blind those around us with the light of God (armor of light)

Skylar Barrett

through the way we live our life, through our actions and through the words we speak.

I like how this verse says, to awake out of sleep. I find that the Lord uses this to be practical in this blueprint for the day. Literally wake up, get your mind going, get your heart and soul awaken to what He wants you to know for the day. The Lord wants us to be alert. He wants us to have our ear tuned to Him. It takes us being proactive and having margin in the day to be still and hear. Waking up early and setting this time aside guarantees that opportunity.

I have started doing as this passage says to do, cast off the works of darkness. I physically dust off my shoulders as an act of removing all the things on my body and in my mind that need to be gone. This physical act is a reminder that right now I need to fight back against the enemy and remove all the things in my life that are not of the Lord.

We are called to be a light in this world, to be the light in the darkness and evil that persists in this life. This is something Christians have always been known for. We sing about in Sunday

26

school, and it's often quoted. But now we are in a time where we need to turn up the brightness on that light, we need to magnify the light, and we need to start blinding this world. We need to be more aggressive and targeting with the light. This verse speaks to knowing the time and that the day is at hand to put on the armor of light. The Lord showed me very clearly a picture of words and actions literally putting people into a mental state of blindness, into a time where people must make a decision on what they think and believe about Jesus. It's no longer time for a soft gospel or a dim light. It's time to dial up the brightness and let it shine.

I challenge you to seek the Lord daily in your actions and in your speech. For me it has been an increasing boldness in speaking about the Lord. It has been in praying for anyone and everyone who needs it, not asking if they want prayer, but either doing it right then and there or quickly following up with them over the situation. It's been an awakening for me, and I have seen great results. More often than not, it's been positive, and people have reacted in turning towards Jesus but there have also been times where that light has turned them farther away. The revelation the Lord has shown me here is that the result isn't what we should be focused on, that's the Holy Spirit's job, but it's the action of shining that light and in this day doing it in a magnified way.

YOUR MOST IMPORTANT OUTFIT

Finally, my brethren, be strong in the Lord and in the power of His might. Put on the whole armor of God, that you may be able to stand against the wiles of the devil. For we do not wrestle against flesh and blood, but against principalities, against powers, against the rulers of the darkness of this age, against spiritual hosts of wickedness in the heavenly places. Therefore take up the whole armor of God, that you may be able to withstand in the evil day, and having done all, to stand. Stand therefore, having girded your waist with truth, having put on the breastplate of righteousness, and having shod your feet with the preparation of the gospel of peace; above all, taking the shield of faith with which you will be able to quench all the fiery darts of the wicked one. And take the helmet of salvation, and the sword of the Spirit, which is the word of God.
-Ephesians 6:10-17 (NKJV)

I find this passage to be an absolute necessity each morning. Just as we put on our clothes for the day, we must put on the armor of God so that we are prepared. As I read this passage, I will pretend to act out putting on this armor, remembering that indeed, I am participating in a war, a spiritual war. I want to be able to fend off the fiery darts of the enemy throughout the day. As a friend of mine told me, imagine you are a soldier waking up early in your tent, putting on your armor and getting ready to take commands from your king.

This passage uses the word stand or withstand four times in just four verses. Therefore, it must be important and significant. Going through this blueprint for the day, the Lord has revealed that He wants us to be aware that we should be standing and ready for battle. The spiritual battle that is happening is not one we are spectators of where we can just sit down. Rather, it's one we are actively involved in, whether we acknowledge it or not. That is why the Lord wants us to be reading this specific scripture every day, because we need to be fully aware that we are in the battle. Too many people go throughout the day depressed, feeling beaten up, tired, and hopeless that they failed in certain areas. You will hear people say that it felt like they went through a war today at work or at school or with their children. Well, that's because they did go through a war, a spiritual war. So, let's change that and let's be prepared for that war, lets STAND up and be ready, aware of what and whom we are fighting against, using the tools and armor God gives us in this passage.

Every morning, I go through each piece of armor, putting it on my body and spirit metaphorically, envisioning in my mind how it will aid me throughout my day.

First, the belt of truth, reminds me I am held together and held up by the truth in His Word, that I am loved by God. That I am saved through salvation and that I am a victor through Him.

Secondly, the breastplate of righteousness, refers to the righteousness bought for us by Jesus at the cross. A breastplate has been issued to each of us who have repented and have accepted the fact that Jesus died for our sins.

It is specially designed by God to protect our heart and soul from all the evil and deception in this world. Our own righteous acts have never and will never be a match for the attacks of the enemy (Satan and his devils). The breastplate of righteousness has Christ's name stamped on it because our righteousness is not sufficient to protect us, so Jesus gave us His.

Third, put on the shoes of peace. He calls us on to be prepared with this peace so that we can call upon the gospel when we need it. Paul, the author of this passage, found protection and strength in the knowledge of what God's gospel and the peace that came with the good news meant for him and for the others he shared with. His footing (his shoes he put on) was sure and unshakable, and he was prepared to carry the gospel wherever God sent him. So, just like Paul, let's not forget our shoes, which supply the peace we need to share His Word when we have the opportunity.

The shield of faith is fourth. What is good to remember here is that we must take up the shield of faith to protect ourselves from the fiery darts. One doesn't wear a shield, one carries, and that is important because there will be times during the day, just as in a battle, that you rest, and put down your shield. But we need to keep that shield close to us, and that shield stands for faith, that no matter what arrow or temptation is thrown at us during the day, we can take up our faith and stand strong, not giving into temptation.

Lastly, the helmet of salvation completes the armor we need for the battle of the day. We need to protect our mind (our head) from the enemy and his deception. We live in a day where there is so much intentional deception aimed at us, often coming in the form of something visual. The Bible tells us in Matthew 6:22 (NKJV) that, "the lamp of the body is the eye. If therefore the eye is good, your whole body will be full of light. But if your eye is bad, your whole body will be full of darkness." The enemy knows all he needs is a crack in our mind or armor to take us down the wrong path, and true to his form, he will always take you further than you wanted to go and keep you longer than you wanted to stay. To combat this, we need to heed Paul's words and guard our mind as he instructs us in Romans 12:2 (NKJV), "and do not be conformed to this world, but be transformed by the renewing of your mind that you may prove what is the good and acceptable and perfect will of God." By renewing our mind, we are protecting it. We need to remember throughout the day that we have eternal salvation through Jesus. That we are His and that He has given us the mind of Christ. We can think like Him and be cunning against the enemy. We have the ability to bring the Kingdom of God with us wherever we go, calling it forth into every situation.

To top it off, God gives us a weapon, the sword of the spirit. This weapon becomes more and more useful (sharpened and deadly to the enemy) through the memorization and declaration of scripture. Reading scripture and the same scripture each day, as this blueprint for the day does, allows God's Word to sink into your heart and gives us the language (our weapon) to declare victory over the enemy during battle.

Finally let's be strong in the Lord and in the power of His might and strength through putting on His armor and taking up His sword. Let's stand and be aware of the battle we are in, so that we can crush the enemy daily.

THE GIFT OF HEALING

who Himself bore our sins in His own body on the tree, that we, having died to sins, might live for righteousness— by whose stripes you were healed.
-1 Peter 2:24 (NKJV)

Heal the sick, cleanse the lepers, raise the dead, cast out demons. Freely you have received, freely give.
-Matthew 10:8 (NKJV)

The verses above remind us that Jesus not only died for our sins so that we may have righteousness but that His death and resurrection has brought us healing to our bodies. Jesus gave us the authority to heal the sick and He wants us healed so that we can then freely give that healing to others. When reading these scriptures, I declare to the Lord and seek healing in my body and for those around me who need healing. I am specific in declaring the healing. As an example, I will say "by your stripes, my wife's sinuses are healed, and she will be sick no more."

The Lord has shown me that He wants to hear specifics from us and He wants to know the details. As an example, if my knee is swollen and throbbing and I have a tear in the meniscus, I don't just ask the Lord to heal my knee. I say "Lord, you love to heal your children and you want to see me healed, will you touch my right knee, repair my meniscus, remove the swelling and give me a quick recovery". The reason I believe He wants us to ask specifically is because He loves us and when He does heal us the way we asked, He alone will get the glory.

Just this past year, I have seen this come to fruition multiple times. This includes my torn labrum in my shoulder. I asked the Lord to fully heal my shoulder so that I would be able to do pull ups and sleep without pain. Now I can do both of those and all the glory is His. This healing of my shoulder came while we were at Mario Murrillo's tent revival in Modesto, California this past spring. I had asked the Lord to intercede and heal my shoulder and while Mario was declaring scriptures of healing over us in the service, a lady walked over to me and placed her hand on my left shoulder and prayed. Immediately, I felt a rush of heat run through my shoulder and it was healed. And that night, I did some pushups and pull ups and was able to hold my wife with my left arm the whole night, with ZERO pain. Amazing! Specific prayer that led to specific healing and all the glory to Him!

The best part of the healing in my shoulder is what happened in the fall of this past year as I was able to see the verse in Matthew 8 come to life. I had freely received healing in my left shoulder, so the Lord wanted me to freely give healing through His power to another man who had severe pain his left shoulder. While we were in Bunnell, Florida at a Friday night service for His Heart Ministries, I noticed a man sitting across me rubbing his left shoulder in pain. I knew right away from the way he was moving his arm and grimacing that it had to be a torn labrum or something similar as I had made those same movements and grimacing faces in the past. At the same moment, the Lord reminded me of these two scriptures and the Holy Spirit prompted me to walk over to this man and pray for the specific healing in his shoulder. I was nervous to do that because what if his shoulder didn't hurt or he was embarrassed by me asking during the service. But the Lord then reminded me of the scripture in Deuteronomy 28 and that I needed to obey the voice of the Lord, so I got up and prayed for him. Lo and behold, this man did have a torn shoulder and had plans for surgery that next week. The Lord healed that man that evening and I was able to hear about it a few weeks after through his testimony to the pastor. A few hours after I prayed, he felt that same heat and was healed, he was able to cancel his surgery. Praise be to the Lord!

What we also learn through this is that sin is a disease, a natural and unfortunate one we all inherited and were born into. Sin, and the symptoms and death that come from sin is the true pandemic that touches all humanity. It ruins our souls and bodies. It causes natural consequences, and eternal ones. The fact that sin is on earth is what causes our natural bodies to experience diseases, sickness, and decay. It brings forth the daily pains many live with. Fortunately, as this verse states, we have a Savior who lived a perfect life, took all our iniquity upon Himself, and removed the eternal consequence of sin. Christ is the true physician, and His blood He shed for us is the balm and sovereign medicine. His blood cleanses us from all sin and it removes the effects of sin as it is the power for healing of all diseases.

I encourage you to meditate on this passage while you read it, write down the effects of the sin in your life that you feel both emotionally, physically, and spiritually. Then thank the Lord for shedding His blood for us and ask that He remove the specific effects of those sins. That He would heal all the wounds you are living with and then after He does heal you, praise Him, testify to others about it and walk in the divine health that He offers us.

LIVING AND IMPACTFUL

For the word of God is living and powerful, and sharper than any two-edged sword, piercing even to the division of soul and spirit, and of joints and marrow, and is a discerner of the thoughts and intents of the heart. And there is no creature hidden from His sight, but all things are naked and open to the eyes of Him to whom we must give account
-Hebrews 4:12-13 (NKJV)

This passage in Hebrews is a great declaration and reminder that what we are reading in the Bible is powerful. It is also just as relevant today as it was when it was written. His Word was meant for me, it was meant for you, it was meant for us, to change our hearts daily.

This passage teaches us that Scripture reveals the current condition of our heart. Once we come to realize that God knows our very thoughts and motives, there is nothing to hide, and after you get past that shocking and scary revelation, it becomes freeing. By reading this each morning and allowing it to uncover our motives, it gets us to the point where we can truly heal.

After some time, the Lord will start to show you what your motives behind your actions and thoughts really are. For me, this has been revealing. For certain actions and areas in my life for thirty-four years I thought I believed and knew why I did things and the reasoning behind my thoughts on issues. However, as I have implemented the routine each morning of allowing space and time for the Lord to work, I am seeing the true intentions of my heart and its debunking earlier convictions and ideas. It's softening my heart for one and secondly, it's giving me the opportunity to replace those earlier intentions and thoughts with God's way of thinking. Which as you can imagine, is a much better way!

IT'S ABOUT OBEDIENCE

Now it shall come to pass, if you diligently obey the voice of the Lord your God, to observe carefully all His commandments which I command you today, that the Lord your God will set you high above all nations of the earth. And all these blessings shall come upon you and overtake you, because you obey the voice of the Lord your God
-Deuteronomy 28:1-2 (NKJV)

But it shall come to pass, if you do not obey the voice of the Lord your God, to observe carefully all His commandments and His statutes which I command you today, that all these curses will come upon you and overtake you
-Deuteronomy 28:15 (NKJV)

I declare Deuteronomy 28 over myself and my household daily. That we will serve the Lord and obey Him and what a windfall of blessings come with that obedience. Then I remind myself that if we are not obedient, again wow, what a windfall of trouble can befall on us. This passage is a reminder that God loves to bless his children but with that He requires something of us as well. Just as salvation (Gods free gift to us) is necessary to enter the kingdom of God, He also requires obedience so that we can receive the fullness of His blessing.

Every other morning, I will read through the entire chapter so that I can truly grasp the weight of this message. God spoke through Moses to tell the people of Israel that they had a choice; be obedient or disobey His commandments. Then He let them know what the effects would be from their choices. God makes it clear throughout the Bible what the cause and effect is from our decisions. He doesn't make His children guess the outcomes and He doesn't force us to be obedient. But like a good father and because He loves us so well and wants us to be blessed, He incentivizes us to make the right choice.

The reasons for the commandments and obedience were so that we as His children would be a highly functioning and blessed people. A people that could resist temptation and being corrupted by the devastating effects of sin and disobedience. A people that could keep families intact, our bodies and minds healthy, our land productive and fruitful, and to keep our society strong.

My advice is to write down the obedience God wants to see, the blessings that come from it and as the curses if we don't. My wife did this and it's something we look at and recite as a family regularly. We have seen this change our mindsets, as well as our children's mindsets and behavior, thus leading towards obedient children and us being able to bless them!

I have summarized it below so you can copy this onto a paper and post it in your house.

Blessings

- Blessed coming in and going out
- Financial Prosperity
- Blessed Health
- Everything you own will be blessed
- Victory over enemies

- You will not need to borrow but you will lend to nations
- Be the head and not the tail

Curses

- Cursed coming in and going out
- Financial Ruin
- Disease and Illness
- Cursed Crops
- Oppression from your enemies
- Be the tail and not the head

GOD'S PROMISES ARE YES AND AMEN, HE STANDS ON HIS WORD

God is so good, and He keeps all His promises. God's word is clear.... His promises are YES and AMEN.

As a husband and father, I find myself in situations constantly where I am promising things. My intention every time is to follow through with those promises, however, too many times I fail at following through. That is why I am so glad that we serve a God who doesn't fail at keeping His promises to us. Anytime I ever start to think that maybe God isn't fulfilling His promises to me, I hear the words that my son, Matthew, loves to remind me of, "God stands on His Word". What a thing to remind ourselves of throughout the day. We should want to live a life defined by His Word not by our experiences.

God's promises are endless throughout scripture. However, the Lord wanted me to be fixed on the following three promises each morning. The promise of receiving wisdom when we ask, the promise of protection over our lives, and the promise of rest accompanied by being released of our burdens.

> If any of you lacks wisdom, let him ask of God, who gives to all liberally and without reproach, and it will be given to him. But let him ask in faith, with no doubting, for he who doubts is like a wave of the sea driven and tossed by the wind.
> -James 1:5-6 (NKJV)

God gives wisdom to all who seek, and He gives it in abundance. This is so important to remember throughout our day. Wisdom is needed in our jobs, in our interactions with others, and in all the decisions we make throughout our day. What has been made clear to me and what I know God wants us to realize is that He wants to give us this insight, His wisdom, and He wants to give it abundantly. All He asks of us in exchange for this promise is that we ask with faith. With firm belief that when we do ask, God will be faithful to provide.

God's promises are Yes and Amen, He stands on His Word.

He who dwells in the shelter of the Most High
Will remain secure *and* rest in the
shadow of the Almighty [whose
power no enemy can withstand].
I will say of the Lord, "He is my
refuge and my fortress,
My God, in whom I trust [with great
confidence, and on whom I rely]!"
For He will save you from
the trap of the fowler,
And from the deadly pestilence.
He will cover you *and* completely
protect you with His pinions,
And under His wings you will find refuge;
His faithfulness is a shield and a wall.
You will not be afraid of the terror of night,
Nor of the arrow that flies by day,
Nor of the pestilence that stalks in darkness,

Nor of the destruction (sudden
death) that lays waste at noon.
A thousand may fall at your side
And ten thousand at your right hand,
But danger will not come near you.
You will only [be a spectator as
you] look on with your eyes
And witness the [divine] repayment
of the wicked [as you watch safely
from the shelter of the Most High].
Because you have made the
Lord, [who is] my refuge,
Even the Most High, your dwelling place,
No evil will befall you,
Nor will any plague come near your tent.
For He will command His
angels in regard to you,
To protect *and* defend *and* guard you in all
your ways [of obedience and service].
They will lift you up in their hands,
So that you do not [even] strike
your foot against a stone.
You will tread upon the lion and cobra;

The young lion and the serpent
you will trample underfoot.
"Because he set his love on Me,
therefore I will save him;
I will set him [securely] on high, because
he knows My name [he confidently
trusts and relies on Me, knowing I will
never abandon him, no, never].
"He will call upon Me, and I will answer him;
I will be with him in trouble;
I will rescue him and honor him.
"With a long life I will satisfy him
And I will let him see My salvation."
-Psalm 91:1-16 (AMP)

God's next promise to focus on is a beautiful one. I love reading this in the Amplified version and the words jump off the page and sink in. This passage has been one that has become so vital to speak over our lives the past two years as we have dealt with attacks on our health. Each morning, I encourage you to speak this passage with true conviction and replace you with and I (or us if you're speaking it over your family).

This passage is a declaration that God wants us to speak over ourselves. He reminds us that He is our provider and our healer. He is what keeps us from troubles, sickness, and death. Yes, we know there are practicalities even safety measures to take and there is modern day medicine but first and foremost there is the protection that God offers that supersedes all of that. Let's review those promises below...

> "I will rescue you..." (deliver, give cause to escape)
>
> "I will protect you..." (set on a high place)
>
> "I will answer you..." (respond to and speak)
>
> "I will be with you in trouble..." (in afflictions, in distress)
>
> "I will deliver you..." (rescue, to bring into safety)
>
> "I will block sickness..." (nothing shall come upon your house)

If we choose to follow and stand on His word in this Psalm, then we get to abide under the shadow of the Almighty or as the Message translation says we get to "spend the night in Shaddai's shadow". I take such peace in this promise. As we have talked about, God gives us choices and one of those choices is where we dwell, where we choose to spend our time and settle our minds and hearts. Too often we choose where and how to do this without much thought. Dwelling mindlessly in front of a television or just sitting in our worries and anxieties. What a disservice that is to our souls, our often-restless souls and minds. Let's take God at His promise and start to consciously choose to dwell in His presence and thus receive the blessing of being in His shadow, of spending the night with Him by our side.

God's promises are Yes and Amen, He stands on His Word.

Come to Me, all you who labor and are heavy laden, and I will give you rest. Take My yoke upon you and learn from Me, for I am [a]gentle and lowly in heart, and

> you will find rest for your souls. For My
> yoke is easy and My burden is light.
> -Matthew 11:28-30 (NKJV)

This promise is one to focus and one that I believe we all need to be reminded of daily. It is an amazing blessing from the Lord. Every time I read it, I take a huge exhale as it reminds me God is in control and He loves to give me rest. He doesn't want me to be burdened with the worries and anxieties of this life. We already know from our earlier scriptures that we are not to be anxious or worry about life, that He will take care of all our needs as we seek Him first. But here, God goes one step further and promises to give us rest and including rest for our soul. What a promise that is to take hold of and lean into.

Every time throughout the day I start to feel anxiety or worry creep into my mind or heart, I go right back to this promise. I take two deep breaths and I read it again. I say, yes Lord, I come to you and receive the rest you promise to give, I take on your yoke, which is easy. It's truly that simple and easy to feel peace and the lightness in our heart, mind, and soul. This isn't a promise that our problems go away or that everything will be easy to handle, but truly I think it's an even better promise. One that says those problems and concerns don't have to consume our thoughts and weigh us down. Because ultimately, we know that God wants to take care of those problems and He will do it in His perfect timing.

So, as you read these promises from the Bible, remember to thank the Lord for being faithful. Declare out loud that His promises are: Yes, and Amen, He stands on His Word.

SING A SONG

It is good to give thanks to the LORD,
And to sing praises to Your name, O Most High;
To declare Your lovingkindness in the morning,
And Your faithfulness every night,
-Psalm 92:1-2 (NKJV)

Oh, sing to the LORD a new song!
For He has done marvelous things;
His right hand and His holy arm
have gained Him the victory.
-Psalm 98:1 (NKJV)

I love to start singing His praises with these two verses above. I declare His goodness as I sing worship songs from my childhood as well as my favorite ones from today. Then as it says in Psalm 98, I ask the Lord for a new song, and I sing that. This sometimes comes in the form of a new poem He will put on my heart. It comes as declarations of who He is, and sometimes it flows out as words in my prayer language.

But stopping to worship Him and to declare his faithfulness over my life is so powerful.

Verse two of Psalm 98 in the Passion translation (TPT) says, "at each and every sunrise we will be thanking you for your kindness and your love". As I mentioned in the beginning of the book, waking up early will cause you to fall in love with sunrises. While you watch a sunrise, you can't but help to recognize God's goodness and beauty. It's in those moments, you find yourself magnifying and thanking Him for all the wonderful gifts in your life. What I love about sunrises is even when I spend those sunrises with people who don't know Jesus, they still end up doing the same thing. They stand there mesmerized by the beautify of it while they are reminded of how grateful they are for the blessings in their life. God is absolute truth, and His creation is beautiful. This stands to be true for all people regardless of what or who they put their trust in.

These verses point to singing praise to the Lord because He deserves it. He is faithful, He has and continues to do marvelous things because through Him we have victory both in this life and for eternity. David, the author of Psalms, tell us to declare His loving kindness every morning. This means to tell God, to remind Him of how good He is, to say out loud the specific things He has done for you. God doesn't need reminding, but He wants it. As a parent, I love and crave when my kids tell me and remind me of the wonderful things, I have done for them. It brings me joy to hear them say it to me over and over. The same goes for God, our heavenly father. He desires and delights in our telling Him what we are grateful for. This is the reason He made humanity. He wanted a relationship and He wanted to be our father. Plain and simple He wanted a family.

HEART SURGERY

Search me, O God, and know my heart;
Try me, and know my anxieties;
And see if there is any wicked way in me,
And lead me in the way everlasting
-Psalm 139:23-24 (NKJV)

After singing a new song of praise to the Lord, our hearts are in a good place for this next passage. Once you are done reading it out loud, take a few deep breaths, really let the weight of the words soak and the ask set in. We just asked the Lord to truly search our heart, to search the innermost parts of our soul so that He would bring out anything that needs to be dealt with, that needs to be healed. We hide things even from ourselves and don't recognize daily what we truly are feeling. This passage is a hard one and it takes time and real work on our part to truly allow God to do heart surgery on us. So, let's give ourselves time here to really pause and take those deep breaths, then come back to this throughout the day when we have time. Create the space and time to come back to this and give the Lord the opportunity to do His work on our heart.

God doesn't want us to be anxious about anything. He makes that clear (Philippians 4:6 MSG) to us throughout the Bible. But why is this? Through getting to know God's heart more, I have learned the answer lies in that He knows what anxiety does to us. It cripples, it consumes us, and it takes too much of our energy. And ultimately, He knows that 95% of what we are anxious about is just a waste of time, as most of those things never even come to pass. He wants to us to be free of anxiety and trust Him. The way to do that is to start to ask ourselves and Him to show what it is we are anxious about. It might be tempting to put this step off in the morning as you don't want to put yourself in that anxious mindset. You have for so long tried to hide those anxious thoughts or been taught to forget about them and just press on. However, fight that temptation, because this process takes time, and the habit building, and discipline is really what is going to heal the hardened heart and allow the Lord to remove the power of those anxieties. Because what is revealed then can be dealt with. As it says in Philippians once we cast our anxieties onto Him, He in return gives us peace.

Reading this passage each morning is our opportunity to declare that our heart is God's. It ensures our heart stays soft and never hardens. We know what a hardened heart does to people (see all of Israel in the Old Testament) and how much God disdains it. I believe that is why the Lord wants us to read this each day, so that we never fall into the temptation or give enough time for our heart to be hardened. God so desperately wants to do heart surgery on us, so let's give Him the chance.

POWER IN OUR WORDS

So then, my beloved brethren, let every man
be swift to hear, slow to speak, slow to wrath;
-James 1:19 (NKJV)

Death and life are in the power of the tongue,
And those who love it will eat its fruit.
-Proverbs 18:21 (NKJV)

These two passages are key to remember throughout the day as the wisdom that pours out from them affects all areas of our lives. I find the words I speak to others and more importantly to myself alter my day more than anything else. Speaking encouragement and truth can sometimes be the hardest thing to do. So, as we dive into this, let's be sure to be, slow to speak and when we do, to remember our words speak life and death. Words are powerful, let's use them wisely.

Swift to hear, slow to speak, slow to wrath.

These words are antithetical to our culture today. We struggle with listening. We are quick to say what's on our mind, we feel entitled to be angry and we fly off the handle too quickly. In fact, the more I think on this passage and how it relates to the time we live in today, the more I am aware of how vital James' words are to us. We have so many more opportunities in this day to fail at this, between social media, our cell phones, and all the interactions we have with people at school, work, shopping, etc.

The great and encouraging thing I have discovered through these passages is that as it says those who love it will eat of its fruit. That saying goes both ways. We have more opportunities to fail but we also have just as many opportunities to succeed. We have the chance to become great listeners, to be slow to speak and slow to be angered and most importantly to speak life (truth and encouragement). Every morning when you read that verse, take some time to think on that, our words speak life and death. That is so important to understand and comprehend, our words are either a weapon or they are a soothing medicine.

Because of reading these verses each morning, I now look at each conversation I take part in as an opportunity to build others up, to be an encourager and to change the atmosphere. As we have learned previously, we are to be the light in this world, we are to be joyful and hopeful, so let's have our words reflect that.

One helpful tool I use to make speaking life and having the ability to be slow to speak a new reality in my life is through writing those words down in my journal. Writing them on the paper next to me while I work, or when I know I am going into a tough conversation. Even writing it on my hand sometimes so that I do not forget. It has made a difference in reminding me, leading to having to do that less and less as it has started to become habit.

PRAYER WORKS

Confess your trespasses to one another,
and pray for one another, that you may
be healed. The effective, fervent prayer
of a righteous man avails much.
-James 5:16 (NKJV)

I love this verse because it speaks to three things we need reminding of constantly. First, we need to seek out those around us whom we need to seek forgiveness from and for those to pray for. Seeking forgiveness daily will keep our hearts from bitterness, which we all know causes internal stress and makes our bodies sick. Secondly, we need to be reminded that our prayers are effective, that bringing all things to the Lord and doing it without ceasing will accomplish much. And lastly, it's all because the Lord has made us righteous through Him. By the time you get to reading this scripture in the morning, you have declared that multiple times.

The power of forgiveness is so clear when we do what the Lord asks us to do. My wife and I have experienced this power often this past year. As we have had arguments come up or when we have hurt each other, since we are both spending our mornings reading through these scriptures, we are so much quicker to seek forgiveness and to give it. It has strengthened our marriage and it has healed our physical bodies as well because we are not carrying bitterness around.

The Lord has taught that prayer is most effective when you commit to it. What do I mean by committing to prayer? I mean it's turning the corner from treating prayer as something you do a few times a day before certain activities or doing it when you need something, to it becoming as natural and instinctual as breathing. It's that important and it's that life changing when you realize that through prayer you're communicating with the creator of the universe, our all-knowing God. And the best fact of all is that He wants to hear from us. He says to bring all things to Him, to release all our burdens and that He will listen, answer, and bless us through our prayer.

Let's dive into a few practical ways to start down the path of making prayer the most vital part of your life. As I embarked on this blueprint for the day journey, I started each morning as I awoke with just saying "good morning and what does the day look like" to the Lord, just as I would to my wife or kids when I first see them in the morning. Yes, that simple.

"Good morning, Lord, thank you for another wonderful day. I am excited for the day, what do you have in store for me today?"

Then as I get dressed and grab my water, I continue in prayer with thanking the Lord for everything I can think of. Sometimes that lasts 5 minutes and sometimes it's just a few things but it gets my heart in the right spot. Then comes the crucial part, where I give every worry, concern, anxious thought, and all my plans for the day to the Lord. I encourage you to tell Him everything, and you will be amazed at the relief and lightness you feel from that moment on. Because as humans we carry too much in our hearts and in our minds that never gets spoken out loud or discussed with anyone and that is not healthy.

Talk to Him about your job, ask Him for wisdom in how you should communicate with your boss, let Him know how worried you are about you spouses' health condition. Tell Him your plans for the day and ask if those plans are in alignment with His will and if not then make that known so you can change your plans. Ask Him for divine encounters, divine conversations, that your eyes and ears are attuned to Him throughout the day so that you don't miss out on anything He wants.

The key here is talk to Him, about everything and throughout the entire day. This is the revelation that I have been given and shown, start the day God's way. Once you start doing this, life changes. Your entire mindset changes in situations, you see your challenges in a new light, you see them as opportunities. You will tackle conversations differently. You will go into your work with thankfulness and looking for ways to improve rather than going in as just another day.

Ladies and gentlemen don't just make today another day. Start it differently, start it with talking to God, talk to Jesus, ask the Holy Spirit for guidance. This fervent prayer and conversation will avail much, God promises that to us. The prayers of the righteous are powerful and effective!

TAKEAWAY OF THE DAY

Keep your heart with all diligence,
For out of it spring the issues of life.
Put away from you a deceitful mouth,
And put perverse lips far from you.
Let your eyes look straight ahead,
And your eyelids look right before you.
Ponder the path of your feet,
And let all your ways be established.
Do not turn to the right or the left;
Remove your foot from evil.
-Proverbs 4:23-27 (NKJV)

The blueprint for the day ends with this passage from Solomon because it encompasses so much of what we have already read earlier. It acts as a battle plan for the day and is a great one to write down on your notebook, on a sticky note, somewhere where you will look at it throughout out the day as a reminder.

Your actions and intentions come from the heart. So, as we know, if your heart is in good shape, your actions will be life-giving, and you will move in the right direction. When your heart is right and pure, you can obey God's word and apply all the scripture we have covered to your life.

What you say over your life depends on what is in your heart. As we know, the power of life and death are in your tongue, which speaks out of the abundance of your heart. Removing all negative and perverse talk from your life makes it so much easier to stay on the right path. As much as it is about speaking life, it's just as important to not negate that with negativity or lies. I have really come to realize that during this journey and in my marriage more than anything else. I can build up my wife day in and day out but if I then turn around and speak disrespectfully or speak death over her, those life-giving words quickly lose their power.

The last three parts of this passage speak to the importance of being ready, prepared and actively engaged in each day. That is what this blueprint for the day is all about. God wants us to live joyful, exciting, fulfilled lives and He knows how that is best accomplished. That is by being in His Word every day. It's through communication with Him. Following His plan and His guidance is what helps us keep our eyes forward and on Him, walking down His path. Once we learn to do that, the benefits of His love and blessings start to reveal themselves daily in our lives.

ENCOURAGEMENT
AND PRACTICALITY

Wake up early, get your body moving, dive into God's Word and spend time talking with Him. Then repeat each morning. That's the blueprint for the day, starting it God's way. It's a simple method, it's a simple approach and it's something anyone can schedule into their morning.

The hardest part about this is the dedication it takes to do this each morning. Because that is where the breakthrough happens. Following this plan each and every day is what will bring about the positive changes in your life. There are practical benefits of starting with a routine. Having a routine is known to be a characteristic of all successful people as it sets expectations for the day and provides stability. Exercising and getting your body moving in the early morning, gives you the kickstart you need to make healthy decisions throughout the day. Waking up early, before most people do, allows you the time to plan which then allows you to accomplish all the other things in your plan for your day.

It's not much of a revelation that waking up early and exercising will positively affect your life, but what is a true revelation is the life changing, life altering benefits that come from spending time in the Bible and in prayer to start the day. As God's Word starts to transform your mind, heart, and actions it changes your life. It makes you a better decision maker, a more productive employee, a better spouse and parent. It produces a healthier body as you learn to grasp that God desires for you to have divine health. You will start to see His promises being fulfilled in your life as you begin speaking life over yourself and your circumstances.

What God promised me and what I am promising you is that following this blueprint for the day and starting it God's way will be a Game Changer! Why? Because this isn't a plan I came up with, it's not full of human wisdom, it's full of God's truth. I am telling you; this will be the morning's game plan I stick to for the rest of my life.

I want to challenge you to pray over this blueprint for the day and confirm it's what the Lord wants you to dive into. Because first and foremost, before you do anything significant in your life such as this, it's imperative you seek God's guidance. But, once you do decide to embark on this, then commit to it for 60 days. Why 60 days, you might ask? It's because after doing this for two months consistently is when I truly started to see the changes in my life. I started seeing the answers to my prayers. It was after those 60 days, that these passages were engrained into my heart which would lead them to pop up in my mind throughout the day when I needed them.

I have included each scripture and, in the order, to be read in the back of this book. Use the margins and space to write down what the Lord is speaking to you. I would use your own journal as well, but I have found it beneficial to be able to carry one book with me that I can read through, take notes in and refer to in the future. Writing down what God is putting on your heart is so important. I was never a note taker, I didn't journal before embarking on this journey and I have learned what a disservice that was. My wife was the one who encouraged me to start with this habit as it is something she has done since her childhood and has reaped the benefits. The act of writing things down and then consistently referring to them drives change in your life and that has been so true for me lately. I am now and will forever be someone who journals and takes notes.

Jump in, join me in this blueprint for our lives. Set that alarm, get out of bed, get moving, grab that Bible and notepad, and most of all expect your day to change. God wants your day to be successful and your life to flourish, He just wants it to start with Him!

SCRIPTURE BY SCRIPTURE

In this manner, therefore, pray:
Our Father in heaven,
Hallowed be Your name.
Your kingdom come.
Your will be done
On earth as it is in heaven.
Give us this day our daily bread.
And forgive us our debts,
As we forgive our debtors.
And do not lead us into temptation,
But deliver us from the evil one.
For Yours is the kingdom and the
power and the glory forever. Amen.
-Matthew 6:9-13 (NKJV)

But seek first the kingdom of God and
His righteousness, and all these things
shall be added to you. Therefore do not
worry about tomorrow, for tomorrow will
worry about its own things. Sufficient
for the day is its own trouble.
-Matthew 6: 33-34 (NKJV)

Be joyful in hope, patient in
affliction, faithful in prayer.
-Romans 12:12 (NIV)

And do this, understanding the present
time: The hour has already come for you to
wake up from your slumber, because our
salvation is nearer now than when we first
believed. The night is nearly over; the day
is almost here. So let us put aside the deeds
of darkness and put on the armor of light
-Romans 13:11-12 (NKJV)

Finally, my brethren, be strong in the Lord
and in the power of His might. Put on the
whole armor of God, that you may be able to
stand against the wiles of the devil. For we
do not wrestle against flesh and blood, but
against principalities, against powers, against
the rulers of the darkness of this age, against
spiritual hosts of wickedness in the heavenly
places. Therefore, take up the whole armor
of God, that you may be able to withstand in
the evil day, and having done all, to stand.

Stand therefore, having girded your waist
with truth, having put on the breastplate of
righteousness, and having shod your feet with
the preparation of the gospel of peace; above all,
taking the shield of faith with which, you will be
able to quench all the fiery darts of the wicked
one. And take the helmet of salvation, and the
sword of the Spirit, which is the word of God.
-Ephesians 6:10-17 (NKJV)

who Himself bore our sins in His own
body on the tree, that we, having died
to sins, might live for righteousness—
by whose stripes you were healed.
-1 Peter 2:24 (NKJV)

For the word of God is living and powerful,
and sharper than any two-edged sword,
piercing even to the division of soul and spirit,
and of joints and marrow, and is a discerner
of the thoughts and intents of the heart. And
there is no creature hidden from His sight,
but all things are naked and open to the eyes
of Him to whom we must give account.
Hebrews 4:12-13 (NKJV)

Now it shall come to pass, if you diligently
obey the voice of the Lord your God, to
observe carefully all His commandments
which I command you today, that the Lord
your God will set you high above all nations
of the earth. And all these blessings shall
come upon you and overtake you, because
you obey the voice of the Lord your God.
-Deuteronomy 28:1-2 (NKJV)

But it shall come to pass, if you do not
obey the voice of the Lord your God, to
observe carefully all His commandments
and His statutes which I command
you today, that all these curses will
come upon you and overtake you.
-Deuteronomy 28:15 (NKJV)

If any of you lacks wisdom, let him ask of
God, who gives to all liberally and without
reproach, and it will be given to him. 6
But let him ask in faith, with no doubting,
for he who doubts is like a wave of the
sea driven and tossed by the wind
-James 1:5-6 (NKJV)

He who dwells in the shelter of the Most High
Will remain secure *and* rest in the
shadow of the Almighty [whose
power no enemy can withstand].
I will say of the Lord, "He is my
refuge and my fortress,
My God, in whom I trust [with great
confidence, and on whom I rely]!"
For He will save you from
the trap of the fowler,
And from the deadly pestilence.
He will cover you *and* completely
protect you with His pinions,
And under His wings you will find refuge;
His faithfulness is a shield and a wall.
You will not be afraid of the terror of night,
Nor of the arrow that flies by day,
Nor of the pestilence that stalks in darkness,
Nor of the destruction (sudden
death) that lays waste at noon.
A thousand may fall at your side
And ten thousand at your right hand,
But danger will not come near you.

You will only [be a spectator as
you] look on with your eyes
And witness the [divine] repayment
of the wicked [as you watch safely
from the shelter of the Most High].
Because you have made the
Lord, [who is] my refuge,
Even the Most High, your dwelling place,
No evil will befall you,
Nor will any plague come near your tent.
For He will command His
angels in regard to you,
To protect *and* defend *and* guard you in all
your ways [of obedience and service].
They will lift you up in their hands,
So that you do not [even] strike
your foot against a stone.
You will tread upon the lion and cobra;
The young lion and the serpent
you will trample underfoot.
"Because he set his love on Me,
therefore I will save him;
I will set him [securely] on high, because
he knows My name [he confidently

trusts and relies on Me, knowing I will
never abandon him, no, never].
"He will call upon Me, and I will answer him;
I will be with him in trouble;
I will rescue him and honor him.
"With a long life I will satisfy him
And I will let him see My salvation."
-Psalm 91:1-16 (AMP)

Come to Me, all you who labor and are
heavy laden, and I will give you rest. Take
My yoke upon you and learn from Me,
for I am gentle and lowly in heart, and
you will find rest for your souls. For My
yoke is easy and My burden is light.
-Matthew 11:28-30 (NKJV)

It is good to give thanks to the LORD,
And to sing praises to Your
name, O Most High;
To declare Your lovingkindness
in the morning,
And Your faithfulness every night,
-Psalm 92:1-2 (NKJV)

Oh, sing to the LORD a new song!
For He has done marvelous things;
His right hand and His holy arm
have gained Him the victory.
-Psalm 98:1 (NKJV)

Search me, O God, and know my heart;
Try me, and know my anxieties;
And see if there is any wicked way in me,
And lead me in the way everlasting
-Psalm 139:23-24 (NKJV)

So then, my beloved brethren, let every man
be swift to hear, slow to speak, slow to wrath.
-James 1:19 (NKJV)

Death and life are in the power of the tongue,
And those who love it will eat its fruit.
-Proverbs 18:21 (NKJV)

Confess your trespasses to one another,
and pray for one another, that you may
be healed. The effective, fervent prayer
of a righteous man avails much.
-James 5:16 (NKJV)

Keep your heart with all diligence,
For out of it spring the issues of life.
Put away from you a deceitful mouth,
And put perverse lips far from you.
Let your eyes look straight ahead,
And your eyelids look right before you.
Ponder the path of your feet,
And let all your ways be established.
Do not turn to the right or the left;
Remove your foot from evil.
-Proverbs 4:23-27 (NKJV)

The author's family.
(photo credit: Matthew W. Kennelly)

To learn more about Skylar Barrett and his beautiful family, visit mustardseedfaithinvestments.com

Printed in the United States
by Baker & Taylor Publisher Services